Workplac

-------Personal-------

Mental Health

Strategies

Strategies on how to Mentally Survive:
the Good, the Bad, and the
Average Day

Table Of Contents

Introduction

Why are we here? Who am I? Where am I going? These are all deep and profound questions that most of us gradually come to at some point in our life. But underneath all those questions, beneath the strife that we endure and the hardships we face; central to all that we do is a desire that seems to supersede all other wants and needs. It is the desire to be happy. Its pursuit is even shrined in the Constitution of this country. We all have the right to pursue happiness because it is as important as living and breathing. If we can't have happiness, then what is the point of it all?

When we are given the liberty to pursue that happiness and we make progress in its fruition, we find that we have a good day. When something happens and it knocks us off our game and we are momentarily distracted from that pursuit, we have a bad day.

Happiness is both conscious in our thoughts and subconscious in our hearts. We mistake some things that can give us this happiness but it's not until it is too late that we find that this fake happiness is significantly more burdensome than we anticipated. Happiness caused by fleeting bliss is never true happiness. Happiness derived from toxins and bad habits enslave us more than liberate us and ultimately give us more bad days than good.

Happiness is best pursued one day at a time. In the pursuit, we find happiness as we make progress on a daily basis. Each day that we progress towards this goal results in a good day; each day we stagnate or fall back results in a bad day in our minds. That is the psychology of good days and bad days.

But that is not entirely true. Good days can be better if we leverage our bad days. Our bad days are days that we think we have not made progress and have fallen back. But that is entirely erroneous. Look at Thomas Edison as an example. When he was searching for ways to make the incandescent light bulb work, he tried numerous times and had hundreds of days where he failed. It was decidedly a bad day when he failed. I say 'bad day' because most people look at failing as a bad thing. But it wasn't. He eventually prevailed because the "thing" that others called bad was exactly what was needed to have that one good day and turned into a success. An entire planet lives off that one good day which followed the hundreds of 'bad' days. That is what I mean when I ask you to leverage your bad days to make your good days more frequent and more prevalent.

We control more than we realize in this life. We control how we perceive things and we certainly control how we respond to things. We make the implicit assumption that all bad days are related to the things we can control. This is mostly true as you will see in Chapter 2, but we shouldn't assume that we can control the things that happen out of random chance. Those circumstances are out of our control, but how we perceive them and how we respond to them can still go a long way in determining if we use it to our benefit or allow it to destroy us.

Bad days are ascribed to everything from bad luck to retribution. You shouldn't see it that way. No one is out to get you. And even if they were, why would you allow them the satisfaction? If someone was trying to make me have a bad day, I would be motivated twice over to have a good one just so I could rub it in his or her face. It all comes down to how you look at it and what you resign yourself to. If you think it is going to be so, it will be so.

We have separated this book into five chapters that cover what it means to have a good day and what that good day should look like. If you define your good day as one that is filled with fun, then you will only have good days when you are on vacation. That would be a miserable way to live. A good day is what your mind thinks is a good day and since you are in control of your mind – or at least you should be, then you should be in control of whether it is a good day or not.

We then leverage your understanding of a good day and look at what a bad day looks like. Bad days are not what you think. Bad days are days that don't go the way you expect them to. The best medicine that I found for that is to expect nothing. Instead of setting expectations, just do what you must do and let faith control the pieces where they fall. You will find that if you do your part, good things that contribute towards your happiness will come your way, increasing over time.

You will then look at the ways that you can actually use the bad days to leverage more good days. You must appreciate the bad days for what they are to do so. Once you get to understand the bad days and how to cope with those, we come to the most insidious kind of days and those are the ones where they are not great, and they are not bad – they are just mediocre days that you feel you are just on the earth and taking up space. Nothing happens, nothing propels you forward and nothing makes you happy. These days are indicative of a bigger problem and you can do a few things to change that – we will look at that in Chapter 4. Then, finally, we look at the best way to put it all together and put yourself on a path to happiness that has a higher frequency of good days, almost zero unintentional in-between days and a reduced number of bad days.

Happy reading!

Chapter 1: What a Good Day Looks Like

Let's be honest, as much as we talk about good, bad or average days in this book, there is really no such thing. The actual day - the one that starts when you wake up and ends when you go to bed for the night, is just the whole world spinning on its axis and facing the sun. Your day is really based on how you see it. You can either make that out as a good thing or take it as a bad thing. You have to make that choice, then decide to follow it.

The day is just the day. Whether it is good or bad is determined by how you see what happens in the day. If you wake up in a bad mood, even the slightest distraction will shake your peace, and even shaky events pass you by and catastrophic events seem more endurable.

It almost always seems that your mood is determined by what happens to you but that is not entirely true. In fact, it is not true at all. If you are willing to take responsibility for how you feel, you will start to soon see more good days than average and bad days put together. The bottom line is that it is under your control.

From this perspective, let me ask you this: When do you think your day starts? Your day doesn't start when the sun rises and you wake up if you really want to take control, your day starts 30 minutes before you go to bed.

There are three things that a person needs to make it a day, and by extension, a good life. The first is that they have to take control of their mind – what they put in and what they broadcast out. The second is that they have to keep their mindset positive. Third, they must come to the realization that everything that happens in their lives is the result of an action or a reaction, and most of the time, it's how we react that determines how much of our peace is shaken.

Let's look at these three things that make for a better day in a little more detail, but we will start with the last of the three – action and reaction. Everything in this world is subject to the forces of action and reaction. No matter what happens in a situation, it is not that which determines what happens to you, it is how you react that has a lasting effect.

If someone is rude to you, you have a number of ways to respond. You could respond kindly, or you could mirror their attitude, or you could do nothing. If you did nothing, it will most likely end right there. If you responded kindly, you could be perceived as a weak person, or if you responded in anger, you could escalate the conflict. The exact consequence of your response is unknown but the fact that cannot be negated is how things move from that point onwards remains exclusively in your hands. You can't control what happens outside and around you, but you can control what is within you and that is enough to control what happens next.

The second of the three is to keep your mindset positive. If you can keep your mindset positive when something happens to you, then regardless of what happens, how you respond will not only determine the rest of the sequence of events but it will also change what happened to you (negatively by most people's accounts) into an opportunity. All things that happen, beyond the norm, are opportunities. You can only see it as such and find out what the opportunities are if you have a positive mindset.

Before we get to the first item on the list that makes you have a good day, let me just take a minute to expand on the concept of a positive mindset. A positive mindset is not what most people tend to think it is. A positive mindset is not about saying everything is good, and everything is cool. That's not a positive mindset, that's denial.

A positive mindset is one that is strong and understands that it is above random occurrences. A positive mind is not distracted or detracted from the momentary glitch in a process, or the delay from forces outside its control or perspective. A positive mind knows that consistency overcomes random occurrence; persistence overcomes momentary glitches, and patience overcomes delays. A positive mindset is not giddy with laughter but mindful with faith that the human body, mind, and spirit, can accomplish anything it desires. So, what is there to be worried about, distracted from, or afraid of?

With that in mind about positive mindsets and the consequence of reaction, we come to the top of the list – the need to control your mind and the will to do it. Controlling your mind is not about telling it to do what you want it to do. Instead, it is about keeping it from wandering aimlessly. When I was young, my mother would keep telling me that an 'idle mind is a devil's playground." Have you heard of that one? As a pre-teen, I had no idea what that meant or what I was supposed to do with that advice.

It wasn't until I got older that it dawned on me what it meant. Having control over your mind is not about the discipline to make it do what you want it to do as much as it is about getting it to stop indulging in things that are not productive or ultimately beneficial towards the purpose-driven life that is a part of all of us.

If I need to read a manual before an interview tomorrow so that I can get a job handling specific machinery, but I can't get my mind to hunker down and read it, that is a problem. If I can't tear myself away from an unsubstantiated fear, then that is a problem. If I can't overpower a habit that is dragging my family and me down, that's a problem. All these situations have a common problem – the lack of ability and will to control the mind. If you leave your mind alone, it will destroy you. Take control of your mind and all good things will fall into place.

So let me pose this question to you, what does a good day look like to you? Take a minute to pause here and come up with your answer to that. When you are done, continue reading. In the next paragraph, I will tell you what my good day looks like.

A good day, to me, looks like any other day on the outside. If the sun is out, that's great. If it's raining, that's great too. I don't let what I can't control bother me, and that includes stubbing my toe, or burning the toast. I don't let what's done dictate what is to come. If I get a speeding ticket on the way to work, I forget that I was stopped by the time I hit the next mile marker.

In May of 2015, I was in Washington for a meeting and was scheduled to return to New York that evening. DC-New York train rides are uneventful at the Acela Corridor. On my way from the meeting to Union Station, there was delay after delay, in everything. From getting to the parking lot, to getting out of the parking lot, then getting pulled over for speeding. The delays mounted and I missed the train. I decided to spend the night in DC and get a morning train back instead. The train I was scheduled to be on derailed after careening at twice the speed limit just outside Philadelphia.

I am not a believer of luck, but I am a believer of good things. If I had looked at all the things that conspired to delay my drive back to the station, it would have been so foolish in hindsight because ultimately all those delays are what saved me from boarding that train.

What does all this have to do with a good day and what it looks like? It all comes together because your good day is with you all day, every day. It is with you because it is in you. You make your day what you will.

Our mind works by association. Have you ever played word association games? If you have then you know what I am talking about. I used to play them with my kids when they were young. Here is how you play it. You sit in a circle and you go around the circle in turn. The first person says a word and the next person says the first word that comes into his or her head, and the next person comes out with another word. The idea is to have the word of the person before you spark a word within you.

The way this works is instructive of how the brain works. Everything in our head works by association. From putting a face to a name to remembering your first date because someone walked past you with the same perfume as your date so many years ago. The brain works by association and when you think of one thing, the brain instantly associates it with something that it had already recorded it with. Because of the way it works, if you see something, smell something, hear anything, your brain automatically triggers an associative memory of other things that have been recorded in your head. From there, that triggers a different memory and on and on it goes. Pretty soon you're reminiscing about rocking horses from grandpa's attic. In the meantime, you have no idea what you are doing or what you plan to do. Sometimes your thoughts can go negative and you could think of all the things that you fear, or all the fearful things that could happen to you. Or the thoughts could trigger into other areas that are fantastical in nature. Whatever the brain conjures is not of concern. What is of concern is that you are not reigning it in. This is the control we are talking about. You must direct your thoughts instead of your thoughts directing you.

We will talk a little more about all this as the chapters unfold.

Whether you are having a good day or a great day, a bad day or a horrible day, it's all in your head. How you perceive it, how you process it and how you turn it to your favor is all up to you and no one else.

So, let me ask again. What does a good day look like to you?

Let's start with that. It should, however, look the way you want it to look. If you decide that the stain on your new tie or the flat you got on your way to work are enough to make it a bad day, then that's what you will have. But if you decide that even getting fired is a great way to spice up your career, then you are in for a lot of good days ahead.

Chapter 2: How to Cope with a Bad Day

There is a powerful strategy I use to handle unpleasant, uncomfortable or just plain painful events. We are only human and there are things that bother us or affect us. The key is not to insulate us from life so that we don't face these things, the key is to fortify yourself so that these events remain isolated. If you receive bad news of something, don't let it alter your state of being so much that everything you do after that is impacted negatively and that causes more headaches down the road.

At the very least, you should isolate those events so that they do not spill into other areas of your life. The strategy is something I learned from Marcus Aurelius. Yes, one of the greatest philosopher-emperors of Rome. In his book, Meditations, he talks about waking up in the morning and telling himself that on that day he is going to meet all kinds of people, the righteous to the unsavory, he is going to fear good things and bad, he is going to face praise and scorn. In other words, anything could happen to him over the course of the day as he interacts with known and unknown elements.

My first reaction to it was that it was a highly cynical way to view life. It wasn't until after some time spent thinking about it did I realize that it is not that he looks at these things as bad or good; but rather he sees that it could happen and that he is raising his soul to meet with these possibilities so that if they happen, he does not entertain disappointment but rather is prepared emotionally and mentally to face them. If he can do that then the moment immediately after the ill event, his frame of mind is not one of disappointment, but one of fortitude.

From then on, I employed this strategy, not to make me feel bad about my day, but to feel invincible. Let me put it another way. Have you ever had a surprise birthday party? How do you remember it compared to other birthdays? I bet you remember it and it makes you feel good, right? It's not the fact that they remember the birthday that causes you to remember it, it's the fact that it made an impact on you. It made an impact on you because you didn't expect it. We tend to remember things that we didn't expect. No, I am not suggesting you expect bad days. I am suggesting that you expect that unplanned things can happen and you tell yourself that you will keep your eye on the ball regardless of unexpected events, unpleasant surprises or failed expectations.

This is the first of the three strategies that you can employ to be able to maneuver around what might otherwise be a bad day. Just like the day began when you went to bed last night. Your mind began this morning with the notion that you should be prepared for the unexpected and to take it in stride.

If a sailor focused on maneuvering each chop and every wave, then it will be a tiring and long journey. A sailor instead has to look at a point on the horizon and as his ship bobs, dips, rocks, and rolls his expert hand dances with the steer without averting his gaze from that point that he has set on the horizon. That strategy builds whatever course-correction you need throughout the day into the task at each moment.

So if you tell yourself that whatever happens on this day, I am going to affix my gaze on the horizon that I decide then no one and nothing can control whether my day is good or bad.

When something unpleasant happens at that point, you deal

with it in stride and then you get back to reaching for the horizon. I guarantee you by the time you get to that point on the horizon, you will feel a lot better than if you languished in a trivial matter with that happened earlier.

A friend of mine called me up in the middle of the work week and said that she wanted to go dancing at that time. It was a strange request, but I complied none the less. We got to the club around 10 that night and stayed until closing time and she spent a total of fifteen minutes off the dance floor. The rest of the night she was moving to the beat. We went for pancakes after and she told me that her father had passed away that morning and she was heading to the airport next to make her flight.

She and her father were always close and one would expect that it would have been devastating. One does not equate dancing with devastation. However, her night out dancing was not celebratory, it was a pick-me-up. She told me that her father had taught her a trick when she was young – "outward action, inward grace" and what that meant was that if she felt horrible inside, forcing laughter or a smile on the outside would gradually beat back the clouds inside. But movement and sweat - dancing all night, allowed her to change the way she felt inside, in preparation to be the strong one for her mother and siblings when she returned home. She didn't feel good because of alcohol; there was no alcohol involved – she was sober as a priest on Sunday. It was the movement she controlled by her physical state.

She left straight for the airport after we ate pancakes and was the rock her family needed her to be.

We all have patterns of how we think we are supposed to act when something befalls us. We fall into that pattern of thinking and looking such a way when negative things touch us. Negative news triggers negative responses by association. It changes our state of being and that in turn cascades into all the things we do for the rest of the day. We go to sleep that night and sleep reset our state of being – for most people in most cases.

Sleep provides us with a natural way to disengage your conscious mind from the problem and that should tell you something. It is your conscious mind that is feeling vexed. Having a bad day is fixed by getting your conscious self to move out of the state it is in. Just like my friend did with dancing, and just like the multitudes of people do when they turn to drugs, alcohol, and nicotine. All these things change their state – and make them forget.

But this is not to be confused with the vexing of the subconscious mind – those times when you feel something is not right but don't know what it is. When your subconscious is vexed, then that is an entirely different matter. That is your subconscious trying to tell you that you are on the wrong path or you need to do something differently. To change your subconscious, you have to do something that resolves the problem.

For now, we will stick to talking about changing a bad day caused by the disharmony in our conscious mind. There are a couple of strategies that come with changing one's state of being. It works well in collaboration to preparing yourself when you first wake up and it has to do with altering your state of being as quickly and as easily as possible.

If you work in an office, make it a habit to go out for lunch. Even if you are brown bagging it, take that bag with you to the park. Get out of the place that you have been all morning and will be all afternoon. When you change your surroundings, you change your state of being. That gives you a new lease on the day and when you head back to the office you will feel refreshed. It's not just the change of scenery that helps with this, but the change of activity that got you there and back. The walk to the park gets your blood flowing and your endorphins streaming. The sunlight changes your mental state and the fresh air perks up your senses like a cup of coffee in the morning. When you put all that together, you find that you are a whole new person. That feeling of being a whole new person is what is meant by the "change of state."

The next thing you need to do is structure your conscious mind into packets of activities. When you are at a task, focus on the outcome of that task and don't think about anything else. Remember in Chapter 1, we talked about disciplining your mind and not letting it wander off? Well, this is the time to practice that. When you tell your mind that you have to do this task and not stop until a certain outcome is reached, then nothing else should pull you away from it. Once that outcome is achieved, then you take a short break and stretch your mind. Walk around the office, go to the restroom, wash your face. It's all a way to decompress your mind before you get to the next task. This is a great way to expand your abilities but at the same time, it works well when you hunker down for at least 20 – 30 minutes at a time. You can't decompress every five minutes.

These packets of activities are not about compartmentalizing your self – this is not about developing your organizational skills. It's about disciplining your mind. When you use these strategies to discipline your mind, you will start to become adept at controlling what your mind does instead of what it wants to do.

Once your mind can do that then you can direct it away from taking unpleasant events and conversations and associating it with bad feelings or feelings of having a bad day. The strength of your mind determines how good a day you have, how many good days you experience and how often they appear. It is all in your control.

If you paid attention, you will realize that we didn't talk about handling a bad day when it happens. That's typically too late. It's like trying to don a parachute after you gall out of a plane. There is a chance you could pull it off but it's going to be extremely difficult. Instead, you have to strap that parachute sack to your back before you get on the jump plane.

In the same way, you have to prepare yourself for any kind of day by strengthening your mind. That was what the first section of this chapter was about. Now we step into the second part of the chapter. Here is when we handle an event or a conversation that would normally lead to unpleasantness.

All bad days come from the same place and follow the same path. There is a trigger, then your mind starts a cascade of associations and then your fear center kicks in and makes you hypersensitive or defensive. At that point, your mind is completely preoccupied and unable to divert processing power to whatever is at hand and so you make mistakes and more errors and bad things follow. It's the same sequence but it may manifest in different specifics. It's not bad luck, but those who believe in luck tend to find ways of working around a bad start.

Here is how they do it – the use some form of a ritual. Rituals work not because it appeases a deity. Rituals work because it alters your state of being and your state of mind. When Alexander the Great (well, before he became great) set out to war, he would do a number of rituals and pay homage to the gods and deities. He won every battle, conquered every tribe, and overcame the largest armies the Persians could muster. Why? Did the Gods help him? No. He won because he changed his state from one of anxiety before the battle to one of absolute confidence by means of the ritual by the time he faced off with his enemy.

Rituals have a way of altering your mental pathways and stirring your mind into the state that it should be. You've seen baseball players do it, even multi-million dollar football players do it. You can use it to work to your advantage as well.

Coping with a bad day is nothing more than compartmentalizing your other activities, disciplining your mind to stay in the moment, and changing your state. You can change your state by using rituals to help you. In my friend's case, her ritual was dancing – it was a physical act that changed her mind set and brought her back to strength.

Chapter 3: Use the Bad Days to Appreciate the Good Days

Nature has a way of stirring things up and calming things down. How you choose to look at it is up to you, but the way I do it is that I take those days that are challenging and difficult to focus because of something painful, or something unexpected by stepping back and thinking that they have their purpose too.

What are the bad days? Are they days that only bad things happen to you? Are they days when a single bad thing that is so large happens that it changes your life? Tell me, right here, mutter it under your breath – What is a bad day?

I have a strategy for dealing with bad days. Well, it is two parts, actually. The first part is that I know there will always be bad days. It's not my job to avoid them or stop them. It's my job to be prepared for them, physically, mentally and emotionally. That's about all I can do. Anything more than that and if there is nothing I can do, well then I step back and let whatever is supposed to happen, happen.

The second part of it is that I take bad days as a means to advance myself. Let me explain. Do you have kids? Do you teach them? Do you do homework with them? Or do you remember doing homework at home? These were never the days that were filled with laughter and exhilaration. It's not like the days you went to Six Flags or Magic Mountain. The typical school day was a solemn affair. What happened on these days? Well, you sat down and did your lessons.

I treat bad days in the same way - they are an opportunity to learn about life. They are conducive to reflection and learning. The harder you fall, the bigger the lesson, the more silent you should be to reflect. I certainly appreciate the good days for all its worth, but I also appreciate the bad days for the things that it teaches me. Life is nothing if not a really good teacher.

We always have a mix of days. Good days, bad days, and days there are neither here nor there. We will get to that last one in the next chapter. For now let's take a good, hard look at bad days.

What do we know so far about bad days? The first thing is that they will always happen and that we just need to minimize their frequency and their impact. We can't abolish them altogether. We also know that bad days serve an important part in our learning process. These days are solemn and reflective and they trigger in us the negative reinforcement of not repeating mistakes. Bad days are not just when uncontrolled things happen in our life but days of reckoning as well. When we do something in the past and we don't know it's wrong, after a few times, we get in trouble for it. Push your luck once, you'll get by; push your luck twice, you may get by; push your luck three times and you're starting to ask for trouble. But if you make a habit of pushing your luck, you start to reap the consequences and those days are hard to stomach.

Bad days come in all shapes and sizes. Some are random. Others are consequences of a mistake from earlier in the day or earlier in a lifetime. You can't choose your bad days, nature won't allow it. You can't choose your bad days because it is not (and it shouldn't be) part of your psyche to look for bad days. Bad days are there to simply teach you.

It may be obvious to state this, but bad days do something important that we do not always realize but always are aware off when it happens. It creates an underlying appreciation for the good days. What happens when you appreciate something? The universe aligns it so that you get more of it. One of the biggest one-two punches you can execute on a bad day is to appreciate the good days and reflect on your bad ones. You appreciate the good days by focusing on them, and you reflect on your bad days by learning your lessons. Most people tend to do the opposite. They focus on the bad days and forget to appreciate the good. This creates a negative feedback loop in your mind.

The human mind is a very powerful thing if you can get it under control, you can direct it to pull anything you focus on toward you. If you focus on bad days, that's what you are going to get. However, when you focus on the good days, you will start to get more of those instead.

Have you noticed that when you buy a new car, suddenly you see more of that car on the road? That's because your mind is now focusing on that thing that you like. If you tell yourself you don't like something you are also going to see a lot of those too – and of course, you have to go through the added effort of avoiding that bad stuff. When it comes to bad days, if you dwell on it and grouch, that's exactly what will happen. You will start to see more bad days. You will always attract whatever you focus on.

Bad days are not really bad, they just feel really crummy. But let's put aside the semantics and look at it for what it really is. Bad days affect us because of two things. On one hand, bad days trigger a sense of fear. On the other hand, bad days trigger an assault on the ego. Both tend to leave us with a vibration that is anxious and unwelcome. We spend the day marinating in that vibration and we chalk it up to being a bad day. That out-of-sorts feeling is also the reason we are overwhelmed and nothing else seems to go right.

Now that you understand the psychological impact and functional use of bad days. Let's look at how you can go about using a bad day to benefit you.

1. The first thing you need to do is act before you have a bad day. Altering the way you think can't happen on the day something goes wrong and triggers a bad day. Instead, you need to look at bad days before they come and, while you do not wish for them, prepare yourself and be wary of your actions so you do not attract bad days which are of the day-of-reckoning type. Rather you only have to end up dealing with bad days that are of the random kind.

2. Condition your mind into thinking that bad days are days where you get to switch to reflection mode. Use the somber nature of a bad day to reflect on the positives of a good day and the benefits of learning a lesson on a bad day. When you were in school, did you learn lessons on days where you were giddy with fun? No, you learned valuable lessons on days that seemed crummy and harsh.

3. Break your mind's habit of over-imagining the negative consequences that may or may not happen when you have a bad day.

4. Do something physical to change your state. Typically, the best way is to do something athletic. My friend went dancing. I typically play a fast game of racquetball as aggressively as I can even if I am the only one playing in the court. That energy gets me to shift from feeling out-of-sorts to feeling clear and energized.

5. Once you change your state get back to the work of that day leaving all the other bad parts behind.

Finally, here is how you use the bad day to your favor. If all else fails, change your scenery. Drive out of the city and find a spot that is near that is surrounded by nature. In New York, that meant heading over to Central Park for me. Something about nature, whether it is the trees that tower above you, the sea that crashes among the shore, or the animals and critters going about their day evaporates all the negative energies that may build up as I try to navigate through tough situations, or whatever it was that constituted a bad day for me.

A really bad day for me meant that something threw me off my game and my mind was just unable to focus – yes, I have those days too here and there. Sometimes, if it is really bad, I stop everything I am doing and change my state by changing my surrounding. I've even gone bungee jumping or skydiving to get a shot of adrenaline or immerse myself in dopamine after a strenuous workout.

The trick is to look back at this statement – "outward act, inward grace." Here is what it means and how it works. If you feel happy inside, you know that you will laugh and feel happy. If you are happy inside, everyone around you will know it because they can see it on your face and demeanor. At the same time, if you feel horrible inside, then it will show on your face on the outside. As you saw in the last chapter, if you force change on your outside, it leverages on your inside and soon enough you start to feel better. What we didn't talk about in the last chapter was permission, and we will talk about that now.

We need to give ourselves permission to be happy all the while when our mind is telling us that we can't be happy in the wake of a certain event. We think (unbeknownst to us) that happiness is inappropriate in certain occasions.

Change your mindset which forces you into being unhappy automatically when something unpleasant happens. It is not you and you are not a bad person. A bad incident is not an indication that you are a bad person, so you must give yourself the permission to act positively.

Permissions are an interesting topic that we do not seem to discuss widely enough in the public forum. We seem to regard permissions as something a higher authority hands down to someone lower in the hierarchy. But in the realm of the psyche, there are many instances that we need permission to be able to function.

There are two mental structures that relate to this. The first is the mental structure of experience. Experience tells us what we can do to expect a certain result or something that we have to do as part of societal norms. The other is the moral structure that tells us what we can and cannot do – but it doesn't have a consequential condition to it. It is something that we are instilled with. To fit in with the society we need to conform to societal norms and being one of the five core fears – where we fear being ostracized from society, we tend to comply with societal norms. One of the things that societal norms tell us is those bad things that happen require us to have bad feelings about them, and that is not true.

Think about it this way. In most western cultures, it is not the norm for people to look happy and entertained at a wake. In some cultures that is the norm. Which do you follow? Which one is going to give you a bad day? It's the implicit permission to be happy in the wake of something that everyone tells you that you should be sad about. There is no right and no wrong answer, and so it is best to do what is best for yourself. Never let anything or anyone bring you down or affect what you are doing next. Mitigate your bad days by trying harder to make something good come out of it.

Chapter 4: The Neither-Here-Nor-There Day

If you can make good days brilliant, and you can make bad days lessons, then what about those days when it's neither one or the other? There are many of these days for most people. If you are one of those people who have many in-between days then there are two things that you can do to change that. But before we get to that, do you want to change it, or are you happy that your in-between days are better than having bad days?

If you have many of these days, then I have to clue you in on a harsh truth. It probably means that you aren't going anywhere. If you are just bobbing along getting on with your day, happy to not make anything of your life, then you are going to have many of these days. Every day that passes you will have lesser chance to make something good. When you do, it will inevitably move from having in-between days to having bad days because one of the things that the body hates more than having bad days, is having non-progress days.

What is non-progress?

Do you know why people get tired of their jobs? It is usually because there is no advancement after a while. Do you know why people get tired when there is no advancement? The reason is that the human psyche is driven by the prospect and experience of advancement. Everything we do has the tendency to escalate because the status quo numbs our senses and dulls our mind. It is in our nature to up the ante as time goes by.

There is a part of us - in all of us, that requires progress to keep us happy. Without progress, we languish in no man's land. It is like getting caught out at sea with no waves, no wind, no paddle and no engine. Once we stagnate, we start to suffocate. The neither-here-nor-there-day is one of those where you start to languish.

If you gave me a choice between an in-between day and a bad day, I'd choose a bad day, because bad days suggest that there is movement and also teach me to learn from mistakes. Pretty soon those bad days become good days. But if you sentenced me to in-between days, then my mind becomes useless, and guess what? It starts to go down its own path and in no time, you will start facing thoughts of depression that will turn your days worse than bad days could ever possibly be.

If you find that you have been having many of those neither here nor there days, and I am sure up to about 60% of you reading this would have, then it is time to take control of your life. There are two things that you should do to change this situation. The first is that you should come to the understanding that you can be more than you are at any given point in your life. If you are a pilot, you can be Captain; if you are a teacher, you can be Principal; if you are a nurse, you can be a Doctor – if you want. What you have to understand from this point on is that you do not have to remain stagnant in anything you do or anywhere you stand.

The human soul is not used to remaining stagnant. All of nature is not designed to remain stagnant – even continents move, vegetation spreads, and species evolve. It is part of our soul to grow, migrate and advance. Under all these changes, we are bound to bump into things, we are bound to make mistakes and we are determined to keep going. If you stop and bury your head under the sand, then you will have plenty of days where nothing happens.

That is a sure fire way to join all those before you that have gone extinct.

This then brings us to the next question. Is having a day like this a good thing where you can just sit back and relax? Yes, of course. But that is only if it happens once in a while. Having it happen all the time is not a good sign that you are living up to your potential.

So how does one cope with this kind of day?

As with all the other things that we talked about, you start by preempting it. You preempt a zero-day by making sure that you are doing one of two things only – you are either in the midst of accomplishing something, or you are resting and giving your body, mind, and soul some well-deserved time off.

If you are in the midst of work and you are having a zero-day then you need to ask yourself why?

I take two days off a week, by obligation. There is nothing you can get me to do in those two days of a week. It is my time to reflect, meditate, do stuff around the house, sit with my family and just let everything decompress and wash away. Even the most ardent power bodybuilders take days off to rest their muscles after a week-long strenuous workout. Even Formula One drivers take a few months off to allow them to rejuvenate. Taking time off is how you up your game. But if you have many zero days in the midst of work, then you have a problem. It is indicative of not doing enough.

I've had people ask me, if off days – days where nothing happens, is so bad, and only good things happen how do I reconcile that? Well, let me tell you. Everything that happens is neither good nor bad. Good and bad are binary ways of explaining things that invoke positive emotions in us versus the things that invoke negative things in us. But we can't keep it at that binary level. My best friend's wife experienced 18 hours of painful labor when delivering their first child. Pain and discomfort are usually enough to trigger a bad day for most people, but not only did my friend's wife go through it, she loved the baby that emerged at the end of that ordeal. She went on to have three more. There are numerous women who go through this kind of pain, but go back and have children after the experience. So, the question is, is it bad, or good? It is whatever you decide it is.

I had an aunt tell me as a kid, that I shouldn't laugh so much (I was a chubby, happy kid). She said that if I were to laugh too much, then later I would cry to balance it all out. I believed her, and I would hold back my laughter so that I wouldn't feel prospective pain later. I opted for neither here nor there all the time instead of the undulating highs and lows of laughter and sadness – good and bad.

Pretty soon, that became the habit. I was more Stoic than I was my natural self always in fear of triggering too much happiness that would then invite sadness. All that was malarkey – I still had bad days. Now, I had given up having good days in return for not having bad days. What I got, instead, was fewer good days and more neither here nor there days and more bad days.

After some time of this, I decided to try a different strategy and I decided that there were always going to be bad days if I defined it as such. There were always going to be good days if I worked at it and there were always going to be in-between days if I did nothing. The one thing common to all of them was that I could control all of it. Even the random bad days where something unpleasant happens out of nowhere.

All I had to do was control how I defined it and how I reacted to it. Remember we talked about the reaction? How you react to something is what matters, not what happens to you in the beginning. To control how you feel in the wake of a random event, it depends on how you prepare yourself on silent days.

You will still have neither-here-nor-there days and that is nature's way of giving you the time to reflect and ponder life and its opportunities. We all need silent time and thinking time but these can't outnumber the good days or the bad days.

A good way to think about the neither-here-nor-there days is to think of them as nature's pause button to direct your mind to contemplation. If that seems contradictory to the first half of this chapter, it's not. The first half of the chapter tries to convey that you have to protect yourself from too many in-between days. Just like you can't work seven days a week, you need quiet days, you can't have a constant stream of good or bad days. Your body needs to stop every now and then.

It is the too many in-between days that will start making you feel like nothing is moving in your life and you start to allow your mind to wander. But if you have a well-measured number of neither-here-nor-there, then what you get is a balanced powerful life. It is something that you should take control of. The days that you take off should be the days that you are quiet. The rest of the days you should be in a state of focused accomplishment.

Let us structure this out a little more so that you get a clear picture of how this should work.

1. Set aside specific days off in the week. In this modern day and age, you should have at least two days off.

2. These two days should be free from distractions of work. Once a week, on one of the two off days, I take

what is called an electronic Sabbath. It is a day that I cut off all gadgets, big and small, and unplug. No internet, no tv, no Netflix, no twitter. I don't even check my email, my SMS, or my phone. I set my phone on silent except for family emergencies and unplug.

3. The rest of the days, I am full-on. I plan my days a week in advance filling it with things I want to accomplish and the tasks that I have to complete in order to accomplish them.

4. I plan my week without regard to random events. This does two things for me. First, to structure my week for getting what I want to be done, and second, it protects me from languishing in thoughts in the event of something unpleasant. If something unpleasant happens on a day that I have nothing going on, it's going to suck the life out of me. If something happens where I must get to my next task, I won't have time to give that unpleasantness the oxygen to grow.

5. Finally, you plan for the good days where you are busy and making progress. After all, progress is the key to happiness and happiness is the mark of a good day. When you don't progress in the way you imagine – whether it is in your studies, in your work or in your hobbies, then it's a day for lessons. You learn about things that hindered your progress.

In the next chapter we will expand this out into routines that you can instill in your life from weekly to daily routines and even annual routines that will lend a little structure in your life so that you can advance yourself, protect your mind and have a significantly greater number of good days compared to bad and the in-betweens.

Chapter 5: End of Day Routines to Have More Good Days

It should be obvious at this point that the whole point about having good days or bad, indifferent days or horrible days is all a matter of perception and response. You have the power to control your destiny if you have the power to control your own mind. The Romans, famous for the conquests and rule, had a very potent saying. *"He conquers twice who conquers himself when he is victorious."*

The saying implies that you should conquer your own emotions even when it is good. There is a twofold lesson in this. The first is that you can tell a man's virtue by how he treats victory. If he gloats and unleashes his desire to thump his chest it is as bad as if he lost because what matters is not one battle, but how a man has control over his mind and his emotions.

For you to control your emotions, the only tool powerful enough to do that is the mind. For the mind to counter the emotions and overcome exhilaration or sadness, the mind needs to be strong and disciplined.

Each evening is a renewal from the wears of the day, and a platform to launch from for the next. It's like the caterpillar tracks of an army tank or a tractor – they connect one to the next and if you keep them moving, then it propels you forward.

The two things that we talk about repeatedly in this book is that you reflect at the end of the day and prepare for the next day, and then you wake up in the morning and you reset your mind to get your day started. That is in essence how you fortify yourself to do things that will result in more good days than bad and significantly less in-between days.

This chapter is going to look at the tools at your disposal to develop your mind so that you can stand strong against any headwind.

1. Have a Purpose

You should always have a purpose and make sure that purpose is far enough out front to create a point on the horizon for you. Like that sailor we mentioned, you have to have a point on the horizon to always align towards, no matter what the distraction.

2. Identify Distractions

When something knocks you off your purpose, treat it as a distraction. This way, it is easy to compartmentalize many of the possible unpleasant things you face. If you only do what you plan toward the achievement of your purpose, then everything else is a distraction.

3. Control Your Mind

Make it a habit to control your mind. If you don't want to think about something, then don't allow your mind to fixate on it. That's a distraction and the worse kind. External distractions can be halted in a short time but internal distractions take time for you to not practice.

4. Renew Your Purpose Daily

As soon as you rise in the morning, bring your mind about by reviewing your purpose and renewing your commitment to that purpose. Remind yourself that you have an achievement to go after. Commit to it and remind yourself that distractions will come, but you have the power to avoid them.

5. Review Your Daily Activity

At the end of the day, once it is all silent in the house and there are no distractions, stand up to yourself in your mind and be accountable for the actions you took during the day.

a. Did you move firmly to your objective and accomplishments?

b. Were you distracted for prolonged periods?

c. Did you accomplish all that you set out to do?

d. Did you spend time with your family?

e. Did you spend time with nature?

6. Workout

Working out on a daily basis is a key to being happy and having more good days. Workouts confer clarity and stamina. This allows you to make better decisions and make fewer mistakes – leading to lesser bad days. Make sure you do at least a small workout just to get your circulation going and get your happy hormones pumping. The more activity you do the better you can control your positive state. The more positive you are, the more things appear positive or innocuous to you. If you are not working out right now, then if nothing else, this is the one thing that you should take away from the entire book. Start working out every day starting with just 10 minutes, and you will notice a significant change in your life. There is no specific time that is best to work out, but the time you work out has different effects. If you work out in the morning, your day will be vibrant. If you work out at night, your reflection period will be clear. If you work out at lunchtime, your afternoon will be energized. Try it out, see which time works best for you.

7. Have a Routine

A routine is like a ritual, it triggers different states within you. The best routine starts in the evening and goes all the way until you get to your first-morning task. As an example, a friend of mine who is highly successful starts his routine at 6.30 pm every evening. It's his cocktail time at home with his wife. They cook dinner together and sit down to dinner with the family. He puts his kids to bed at 9 and heads to the study and starts at 9.30 on the dot. Here he reflects on his day. He makes notes of points that occur to him about it. He analyzes conversations he had, makes notes about where he can improve and then looks at the things he needs to do the following day. He has two lists – a task list and an accomplishment list. (Task lists are things that he has to do with instant outcomes. For instance – a task to go to the laundry place on the corner can be easily accomplished and the objective and the accomplishments are very close to each other. These tasks are easily accomplished. The second is the list of accomplishments that you want to make but you don't break them down into tasks. You focus on the objective and let your task for the moment be dictated by the desire to do whatever it takes.) Once he has done that, he visualizes the accomplishment of those lists and goes to bed. When he wakes up, before even opening his eyes, he searches and locates in his mind all the things he had visualized the night before and gets into character for the day. He puts himself in a state, gets out of bed and starts going after what he has to do. From the 6.30 pm to 4.30 am (did I mention he wakes up at 4 am?) everything is scripted into a habitual routine.

8. Wake Up Early before the Sun Rises

Start your day before everyone else in the house and before the sun illuminates the sky. Remember to prepare yourself for the unexpected and remind yourself to use the schedule and purpose on the horizon to protect and shield you from distractions.

9. Meditate

People tend to get turned off at the mention of meditation. It's not what you think. I am not suggesting that you take up meditation in any spiritual sort of manner. This is a comparatively mild version of meditation when you clear your mind and just allow it to decompress. You focus on the silence and away from the chaos.

10.   Read

The idea of reading is almost too trivial to mention but it needs to be included in your daily evening routine. The topic of your reading should stay away from things like world news or anything negative. You should read anything that you like as long as it contributes to building you up rather than breaking you down.

These ten items will serve you well as you do them on good days, bad and the days that fall in between. If you do these as a ritual then it will gradually become the precursor to a driven self. Starting the night before allows your subconscious to prepare you through the night then fire you up again in the morning when you wake up. It is the best thing that has worked for me in my life, and I notice that a lot of successful people have some similar routines where they let their subconscious do the heavy lifting at night while they sleep than when they wake up. It seems that they have made things easier for themselves.

You can arrange these ten steps in any arrangement you'd like, as long as it makes sense to you and your lifestyle will create a path to more happy and good days.

As you assimilate all this, there are a few other issues that you should keep at the back of your mind. The first is that the body needs to have two parts in balance. It needs work and it needs rest. You can't have all work and no rest, and you can't have all the rest you'd like and no work. You need both, and it is as important as each other. While they are equally important, their quantity, measured in time, is not equal. You don't have 6 hours of work followed by 6 hours of play or rest. They vary by individual and you need to find the ration that optimizes your performance. For me, I find that five hours of sleep at night works ideally when I supplement it with a quick 10-minute snooze at lunchtime. I am equally fresh after lunch in that case as I am when I first wake up. A large part of having a good day is to keep the mind well rested. So, take the time to rest and take the time to de-stress and unwind in the evening when you get home. If you have the opportunity to stop at the gym, that would be a good way for you to wind down.

You should also practice good eating habits. If you are carrying an extra load in terms of weight, you should consider doing something about it. Eat healthily but don't starve. Adopt and maintain good eating habits and let your body weight return to normal using a good workout routine. The increased endorphins from the workout and the reduction in toxins from eating healthy will go a long way in giving you clarity of mind and that will make for many good days.

Most importantly, the key to having good days and increasing their frequency is to have a formidable support structure. Not only does it give you purpose but it also provides you with an outlet to talk about things – not just problems but of the good things and the fun things.

The key is to keep your family close. Sometimes we forget that our families are the best things that happen to us. They give us all we need and demand nothing in return. The days you get to spend with your family are always good days if you so choose to decide.

With all that said and done, it's time to look at a simple routine at the end of each day that will be certain to align the stars in your favor so that you wake up ready to take on your accomplishments.

1. Workout before dinner

2. Have a light dinner with family

3. Spend some time playing games or chatting with your family

4. Read something that interests you

5. Listen to classical music

6. Meditate

7. Reflect and review your day

8. Plan your next day

9. Go to bed by 10pm

Make this simple list into a habit and you will start to see the benefit in terms of good days within a week of practice.

Conclusion

Now that you understand how to differentiate a good day from the bad and you have a few tricks in your bag to convert a bad day to good and a good day to great by changing your appreciation of it and your perception of what an event means.

At the end of the day, it all really is in your head, and how you react from that point on. In this book, we talk frequently about purpose and goals and there is an implicit bias towards leading a successful life. But the thing to note is that success is not always about money. Of course, you could live a life that is rich if you so desire but that is not the definition of happiness. In fact, in some cases, too much money and material wealth tend to take away from having a good day and increase your bad days if you mess up the reason behind the wealth. Success is about reaching for your purpose and if you can identify your purpose and move toward it, happiness tends to roll in the same direction. As your mind and subconscious know you are moving in a positive direction you have a good day and your perception of all things changes.

Perception moves along two directions. You can use perception to have a good day by perceiving things in a good way, or you can have a really good day and thereby perceive things positively – which then compounds your good day.

Embrace your good days and cradle your bad ones. Bad days are not bad nor intended to punish you. You should step away from any notion that bad days, whether random or consequential, have anything to do with punishment. They don't and in fact, they have more to do with your future betterment and the way that nature teaches you to stop and go a different path. Bad days are about building and correcting and you need those days. The moment you can look at a bad day and see it as an instrumental part of the whole, you will start to leverage those bad days by learning from them so that you can have more good days.

A funny thing happens when we start to see bad days as road signs to go the right way. We start to see them as a different kind of good day. Even the random bad days start to have meaning. When I missed the train to New York, I was in the midst of having, what most people would call, a bad day. I was running late, people were stopping to talk to me, then I got pulled over, and had to spend the time getting a ticket. All of which made me late and feel out-of-sorts in a way. Missing that train felt like a really bad day until I found out about the wreck. Suddenly it felt like the best thing that happened to me.

From that day on I started to really appreciate the things that happen but initially thought about it as bad. I started to look for the good in everything that happened. Whether that was the right or wrong thing to do didn't matter because that decision to see everything positively changed my life.

The days that really languish for most people are the neither-here-nor-there days. It's not a good day and it's not a bad day. We saw that chapter in this book and we've all had these days. I don't have those anymore. I schedule those days now – they are my Stoic days – days where I intentionally keep everything quiet. You can think of those days like you would a phone. If you don't periodically charge your phone, you run out of juice and you have to have downtime while the phone charges. But if you schedule the down time and let the phone charge up then there is neither-here–nor-there days. It is what I call in-between days because they are in between unexpected downtime.

Whatever you take from this book just remember that your day is how you think of it at the moment, how you prepare for it ahead of time and how you reflect on it when it passes. It is a dynamic process that you have to keep at as a lifestyle and not a fad that you drop off after some time when things start going well for you.

All the things we talked about in this book are designed to keep you reaping more benefits from your day and by coping with the day with real strategies not just band-aids to cope superficially.

Your workplace can be highly stressful because it offers all the things that you need to define your day. It can offer you progress to make your day good. It can offer you challenges and random failures that can make it worse, or it can drag and be unworthy of your attention. But however the environment handles your day, you have the last word on how you perceive it and how you react to it.

Make sure you step away from the office or the workplace and go for a walk or go for a drive. Set foot amidst nature and take everything in stride. The good, the bad and the indifferent are merely different and diverse blocks that make up the structure of your happiness and your pursuit of it will go much better if you perceive it in a way that benefits you rather than alarms you.

Made in the USA
Middletown, DE
06 August 2019